# WHOSE EARS?

by

Rebecca Phillips-Bartlett

Minneapolis, Minnesota

**Credits**
Images are courtesy of Shutterstock.com. With thanks to Getty Images, Thinkstock Photo, and iStockphoto. Cover – StockSmartStart, Vladislav T. Jirousek, Japan's Fireworks, 2630ben. 2–3 – Jurie Maree, Elizabeth Caron. 4–5 – les images, Rastkobelic. 6–7 – Eric Isselee, R J Endall Photographer, Thomas Retterath, Marko Bowman, Zvereva Yana, GoodStudio. 8–9 – AB Photographie, Vladislav T. Jirousek. 10–11 – Andrea Izzotti, Crystal Alba, Eric Isselee, Rebius, Sfax D.C, LAN02, RioRita. 12–13 – Felineus, slowmotiongli. 14–15 – CezaryKorkosz, DOME PRATUMTONG, reptiles4all, Yatra4289, Sazid Zubaer, Elena Khmelniuk. 16–17 – Geza Farkas, Martin Janca, jbmake. 18–19 – cmmedia99, Fercast, Philippe Clement, Zety Akhzar, Tartila. 20–21 – Kurit afshen, Kurit afshen. 22–23 – Pooja Prasanth, rameesha thisarindu, Sergey Uryadnikov, Sourabh Bharti, Victoria Chudinova.

**Bearport Publishing Company Product Development Team**
Publisher: Jen Jenson; Director of Product Development: Spencer Brinker; Managing Editor: Allison Juda; Editor: Cole Nelson; Associate Editor: Naomi Reich; Associate Editor: Tiana Tran; Art Director: Colin O'Dea; Designer: Kim Jones; Designer: Kayla Eggert; Product Development Specialist: Owen Hamlin

*Library of Congress Cataloging-in-Publication Data*

Names: Phillips-Bartlett, Rebecca, 1999- author.
Title: Whose ears? / Rebecca Phillips-Bartlett.
Description: Minneapolis, Minnesota : Bearport Publishing Company, [2025] | Series: Can you guess? | "Fusion books."
Identifiers: LCCN 2024035368 (print) | LCCN 2024035369 (ebook) | ISBN 9798892327350 (library binding) | ISBN 9798892327855 (paperback) | ISBN 9798892328227 (ebook)
Subjects: LCSH: Ear--Juvenile literature. | Animals--Juvenile literature.
Classification: LCC QL948 .P45 2025 (print) | LCC QL948 (ebook) | DDC 591.4/4--dc23/eng/20240810
LC record available at https://lccn.loc.gov/2024035368
LC ebook record available at https://lccn.loc.gov/2024035369



For more information, write to Bearport Publishing, 5357 Penn Avenue South, Minneapolis, MN 55419.

# CONTENTS

# WHOSE EARS COULD THESE BE?

Ears help animals know about the world around them. But can you guess an animal just from its ears? Whose ears could those be sticking out of this tall grass?

What can ears tell us about an animal?

They are a **RABBIT'S** ears!

On the following pages, you will see photos of some ears and three different animals. Look at the pictures and read the clues to guess whose ears are shown. Then, turn the page to find the answer.

# A POINTY PAIR OF EARS

Below is the first pair of ears. What do you notice about them?

These ears are very big. Maybe this animal has good hearing?

The ears are also very thin. This might help an animal keep cool. Which animals need help staying cool?

Whose ears could these be? Choose which animal you think best fits the ears.
Kangaroo
Aardvark
I like to roll in mud to stay cool.
Pig

# WHOSE EARS ARE THEY?

They are the **AARDVARK'S** ears!

Don't make so much noise . . . I'm trying to listen!

Aardvarks are **mammals** that live mostly in the savannas and grasslands of Africa. An aardvark's large ears help it stay cool in the African heat.

Aardvarks are nocturnal, so they are mostly awake at night. This is when they hunt ants and termites. Aardvarks can't see very well, so they use their ears to listen for **predators** while they hunt.

Aardvarks use sharp claws to dig underground **burrows**.

These animals stay in their burrows to avoid the heat during the day.

# FANCY, FURRY EARS

Here is another pair of animal ears. Whose could they be?

The black tufts of fur on top of these ears make the animal look like it's wearing a crown!

Most of the animal's head is a sandy color. This could help **camouflage** the creature.

Which of these animals might have ears like this? Choose one.
Dog
Caracal
I look so fancy!
Squirrel

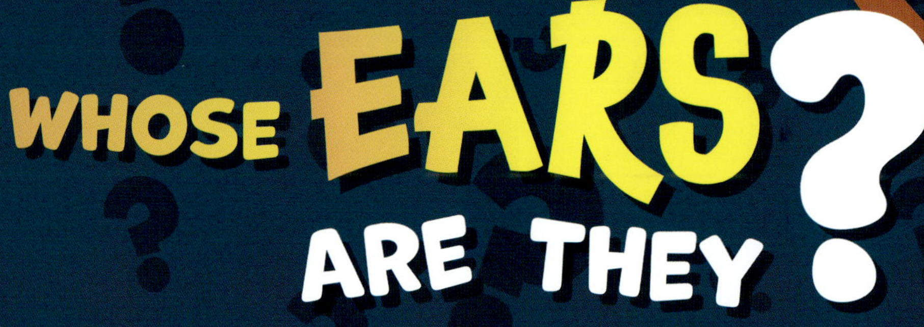

# WHOSE EARS ARE THEY?

They are the **CARACAL'S** ears!

Do you think they got it right?

I hope so!

Some scientists think the caracal's cute ear tufts help these wild cats by sensing distances or discovering things in their paths. Others think tufts may help caracals recognize one another.

A caracal's ear has 20 **muscles**. This helps it turn its ears to hear sounds in all different directions. Great hearing makes caracals excellent hunters.

Sometimes, a caracal's ear tufts droop as it gets older.

Caracals use their pee and poop to mark their **territory**.

# BOWL-SHAPED EARS

Here are the next pair of animal ears. What can their shape tell us?

These ears are big and rounded.

The ears are also very thin.

These ears look a bit like a bowl with ridges inside. The shape gathers sounds so the animal can hear very well.

Whose ears could these be? Here are three animals to choose from.
Bat
Koala
How is my hat staying on?
Jerboa

# WHOSE EARS ARE THEY?

They are the **BAT'S** ears!

I'm just hanging around. . . .

These mammals use their ears for **echolocation**. First, a bat sends out a sound that bounces off things around them. Then, the sound comes back to the bat's ears as an echo.

Bats use the echoes to know what's around them and to find their **prey**. A bat's ears are very good at picking up other sounds. They can even hear the fluttering of a moth's wings!

Different kinds of bats have different sizes of ears. Some kinds have ears nearly as long as their bodies!

Many kinds of bats can't see very well.

# NO-FLAPS EARS

Here's another animal . . . but where are its ears?

This animal doesn't have ear flaps that stick out or stand up. It just has a flat area on either side of its head.

The area around the ear is covered in green scales.

Whose unusual ear could this be? Make a choice from the following animals.
Alligator
Don't come too close or I'll bite!
Lizard
Tortoise

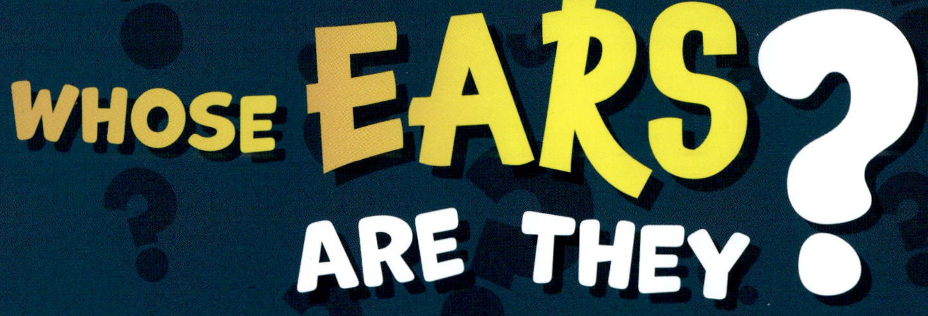


They are the **LIZARD'S** ears!

My ears may look different, but I can still hear you talking about me!

Lizard ears work in a way similar to a human's. Sound **vibrates** a bit of skin stretched across the ear opening. This moves small body parts underneath, and the lizard hears the sound.

Lizards are **reptiles** that eat mostly insects. They hunt by staying still and waiting. They use their ears to listen and their sharp eyes to look for their prey.

Crocodiles can hear about as well as lizards. Snakes and turtles are better at feeling vibrations in the ground.

Some lizards live mostly underground. Their ear openings may be covered by scales.

# BONUS EARS

An elephant's huge ears are good at hearing and help the animal stay cool. The size of an elephant's ears can tell you where it's from. African elephants have much larger ears than their cousins from Asia.

## ENORMOUS EARS!

The ears of the largest elephants can grow up to 6 feet (1.8 m) wide!

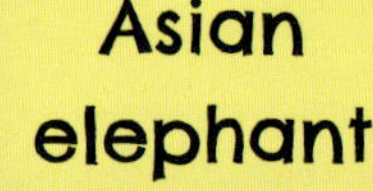

# THREE CHEERS FOR EARS!

There are so many kinds of animal ears, from bowl-shaped to furry, fancy crowns. These ears help creatures stay safe, find food, and learn about their world. How do your ears help you?

# GLOSSARY

**burrows** homes that animals dig in the ground

**camouflage** to hide by blending into the surroundings

**echolocation** a method of sensing the environment by using sound and echoes

**mammals** animals that have hair or fur and drink their mothers' milk as babies

**muscles** the parts of the body that allow it to move

**predators** animals that hunt other animals for food

**prey** animals that are eaten by other animals

**reptiles** cold-blooded animals that have scaly skin

**territory** an area of land that belongs to an animal

**vibrates** shakes quickly

# INDEX